Sports Illustrated KIDS

Football GOATs

The Greatest Athletes of All Time

BY BRUCE BERGLUND

CAPSTONE PRESS
a capstone imprint

Published by Capstone Press, an imprint of Capstone
1710 Roe Crest Drive, North Mankato, Minnesota 56003
capstonepub.com

Library of Congress Cataloging-in-Publication Data
Names: Berglund, Bruce R., author. Title: Football GOATs : the greatest athletes of all time / by Bruce Berglund. Other titles: Football greatests of all time
Description: North Mankato, Minnesota : Capstone Press, [2022] | Series: Sports illustrated kids. GOATs | Includes bibliographical references and index. |
Summary: "How do you pick football's GOATs? Is Tom Brady the greatest quarterback? Is Alan Page the greatest defensive tackle? Who's the all-around champ? It comes down to stats, history, and hunches. Read more about some of the legends of football and see if you agree that they're the greatest of all time"— Provided by publisher.
Identifiers: LCCN 2021042790 (print) | LCCN 2021042791 (ebook) |
ISBN 9781663976369 (hardcover) | ISBN 9781666321623 (paperback) |
ISBN 9781666321630 (pdf) | ISBN 9781666321654 (kindle edition)
Subjects: LCSH: Football players—Biography—Juvenile literature. | Football—Records—Juvenile literature. | Football—Statistics—Juvenile literature.
Classification: LCC GV939.A1 B43 2022 (print) | LCC GV939.A1 (ebook) | DDC 796.33092/2 [B]—dc23
LC record available at https://lccn.loc.gov/2021042790
LC ebook record available at https://lccn.loc.gov/2021042791

Editorial Credits
Editor: Ericka Smith; Designer: Sarah Bennett; Media Researcher: Svetlana Zhurkin; Production Specialist: Katy LaVigne

Image Credits
Alamy: Niday Picture Library, 5 (left); Associated Press: 10, David Durochik, 21 (right), Harold P. Matosian, 14, Paul Spinelli, cover (bottom left), 23, Peter Read Miller, cover (bottom right), 7 (top), Richard Drew, 19 (top), Tony Tomsic, 26; Newscom: UPI/Bill Pugliano, 27, UPI/Steve Nesius, 5 (right), ZUMA Press/Al Golub, 15; Shutterstock: Apostle (star background), cover, back cover, and throughout, Sunward Art (star confetti), 4, 6, 20; Sports Illustrated: Al Tielemans, 8, 12, 29 (top), Bill Frakes, 21 (left), Bob Rosato, 11, 17, David E. Klutho, cover (bottom middle), John Biever, cover (top left and top right), 19 (bottom), 22, John Iacono, cover (top middle), 13, John W. McDonough, 25 (bottom), Peter Read Miller, 16, 25 (top), Robert Beck, 9, 29 (bottom), Walter Iooss Jr., 7 (bottom)

All records and statistics in this book are current through the 2020 NFL season.

Printed and bound in China. 6667

Table of Contents

Words in **bold** appear in the glossary.

How to Pick Football's Greatest

The idea behind the game of football is simple: One team tries to get the ball to the end of the field and score. The other team tries to stop them.

The details of the game are more **complicated**. Coaches in the National Football League (NFL) call different **formations** and plays. There are different positions on offense and defense. And each position has special jobs. A quarterback is different from a linebacker. An NFL team needs them both.

In the same way, when we choose football's GOATs—the greatest of all time—we have to pick quarterbacks and linebackers, as well as wide receivers, defensive ends, and more. Who would you pick?

The NFL is just over 100 years old. Jim Thorpe was the best player when the league started. He played both offense and defense. He ran the ball, threw passes, and kicked field goals. He also played professional baseball and won two Olympic gold medals.

Most NFL players today play only one position. Patrick Mahomes, though, throws and runs for touchdowns, like Jim Thorpe did. Mahomes is also a great all-around athlete. He could have played professional baseball but chose football instead.

Defense

Defensive Tackles

The job of the defense is to stop the other team from scoring. You need big, strong players to hold the **line of scrimmage** and keep the offense from gaining yards.

Two of the greatest defensive tackles played in the 1970s—Alan Page and Joe Greene. Their teams had strong defenses. Page was so important for the Vikings that he was named the NFL's Most Valuable Player (MVP) in 1971. He was the first defensive player ever to win the award.

Greene led the Steelers to four Super Bowl wins. In 1976, the Steelers' defense shut out other teams five times—an NFL record tied with the 1944 New York Giants. That season, the Steelers gave up, on average, fewer than 10 points per game. Only four other teams in NFL history have done that. One of those teams was the Vikings—led by Alan Page.

Page studied law while playing with the Vikings. He later was a judge on the Minnesota Supreme Court.

Greene was one of the most famous football players in the NFL. He even acted in commercials and movies. Everyone called him “Mean” Joe Greene.

Defensive Ends

Defensive ends stop the offense from running the ball outside. They have to be big and strong to fight off blockers. They are also fast. On passing plays, defensive ends race in to get the quarterback. If they tackle the quarterback behind the line of scrimmage before he throws the ball, they get a sack.

Reggie White was so strong he could throw blockers to the ground with one arm. He has the second-most sacks in NFL history. In the fourth quarter of Super Bowl XXXI, White sacked the Patriots' quarterback three times. The sacks helped keep the Patriots from scoring, and the Packers won the game.

White in a game against the Tampa Bay Buccaneers in 1998

Watts tries to get past a Chicago Bears player during a game in 2016.

Growing up in Wisconsin, J.J. Watt watched Reggie White lead the Packers to the Super Bowl. When Watt reached the NFL, he studied his hero's moves. But Watt says he still can't throw blockers to the ground with one arm. That's too amazing even for him. But both players make the GOATs list for many fans.

Comparing White and Watt

How do White's and Watt's first 10 seasons match up?

	Reggie White	J.J. Watt
Games	153	128
Sacks	145	101
Forced Fumbles	23	25
Defensive Player of the Year Awards	1	3

Inside Linebackers

Inside linebackers get ready behind the defensive tackle. They stop running backs, cover receivers in the middle of the field, and sometimes **blitz** to sack quarterbacks.

Dick Butkus and Ray Lewis are the greatest inside linebackers of all time. Both players were strong, fast, and **fearsome.** They could make tackles all over the field. They were quick enough to cover receivers and **intercept** passes. They would hit the running backs so hard they would knock the ball loose for a fumble.

Dick Butkus

The best linebackers in high school, college, and professional football receive the Butkus Award.

Lewis holds the NFL records for most tackles in a season and most career tackles. He was the MVP of Super Bowl XXXV in 2001.

When athletes are standout players, their teams might put statues up in their honor. Butkus and Lewis have statues in their honor outside the stadiums where they played—either in college or professionally.

Outside Linebackers

Outside linebackers cover the sides of the field. They can be reliable players who stop running backs, cover receivers, and intercept passes. They can also be exciting players who blitz the quarterback and get sacks.

Derrick Brooks was the best at stopping a run. He tackled offensive players all over the field. He also covered receivers and intercepted passes. Brooks returned six interceptions for touchdowns—tied with Bobby Bell for the all-time record for linebackers.

Lawrence Taylor was an outside linebacker who blitzed into the offense's backfield. He sacked the quarterback and knocked the ball out of running backs' arms game after game.

Brooks tackles a running back during Super Bowl XXXVII.

Taylor was the second defensive player to win the NFL MVP award.

Two Different Linebackers

	Derrick Brooks	Lawrence Taylor
Seasons	14	13
Tackles	1,713	1,088
Sacks	13.5	132.5
Forced Fumbles	24	33
Interceptions	25	9
Touchdowns	6	2

Cornerbacks

Cornerbacks are fast. They have to run down the field with the wide receiver, step for step. They break up passes and try to intercept the ball.

One great player shaped the way all cornerbacks play. His name was Dick Lane, but everyone called him "Night Train." In his **rookie** year, Lane intercepted the ball 14 times in a season of just 12 games. In 1978, NFL teams began playing 16 games each season. But no one has broken Lane's record.

When Lane retired in 1965, he had a total of 68 interceptions. That is still the fourth highest number in NFL history.

Sanders (right) returned punts and kicks.

Deion Sanders never led the league in interceptions. That's because quarterbacks wouldn't throw to his side of the field. He was known as a "shutdown" cornerback. Because he was so fast, he would shut down the offense's best receiver.

Safeties

Safeties line up about 10 or 15 yards from the line of scrimmage, behind the linebackers. They rush forward to stop running backs and drop back to cover wide receivers. Safeties are the last wall of defense. Nobody should get past them. So they have to be fast and good tacklers.

Ronnie Lott and Ed Reed were both great tacklers. And they were feared as hard hitters. They would bring down running backs and receivers anywhere on the field. Lott had 1,146 tackles in his **career**.

Lott was the leader of the 49ers' defense when they won four Super Bowls.

Reed holds the NFL record for longest interception return. He caught the ball in his own end zone and ran 107 yards for a touchdown.

Lott and Reed were also called "ball hawks." If there was a passing play, they would come out of nowhere to attack the ball in midair, like a hawk attacking its prey. Both players are in the top 10 for most career interceptions. Reed had 64 interceptions, and Lott had 63 interceptions.

Special Teams

Kickers & Punters

Kickers knock the ball through the goal posts for field goals and extra points. Punters kick the ball to the other team when the offense is stopped. In the early days of the NFL, players like Jim Thorpe kicked and punted. Now, teams have players whose only job is kicking or punting.

The greatest punter ever is Ray Guy. His punts stayed in the air a long time, so his teammates could run down the field and keep the other team from returning the ball. The coach of another team thought that Guy's punts went so high because he was cheating. He checked to see if Guy filled the football with helium, the gas that makes balloons float. But he found no evidence of helium in the football.

Adam Vinatieri is the greatest kicker of all time. He holds the NFL records for most field goals and most points scored. He is most famous for his game-winning field goals, especially in the playoffs.

During the 1976 Pro Bowl, Guy once punted the ball so high it hit the scoreboard at the Superdome in New Orleans—90 feet above the field.

Vinatieri kicked last-second field goals to win Super Bowl XXXVI and Super Bowl XXXVIII.

Offense

Linemen

At the start of every play, the ball snaps and the offensive linemen spring into action. On running plays, the linemen open space for running backs. On passing plays, they give the quarterback time to find a receiver.

Bruce Matthews played every position on the line. He was a tackle—the player who protects the quarterback from defensive ends and outside linebackers. He was a guard, who runs downfield to block for running backs. And he was a center, who snaps the ball and battles defensive tackles. Matthews was great at every position.

But the greatest lineman of all was Anthony Muñoz. He played left tackle—the most important position on the line. Muñoz had to protect the "blind side," the side of the field the quarterback can't see when he drops back. Muñoz used speed and balance to protect the blind side. He also used strength to open space for running backs.

Matthews started 293 games. That's more than any lineman ever and third most for any player in NFL history.

Muñoz was known for getting "pancakes." That's when a lineman blocks a defensive player and knocks him to the ground, making him flat as a pancake.

Sizing Them Up

Football players are different sizes, depending on their position.

Player	Position	Height	Weight (pounds)
Ronnie Lott	Safety	6'0"	200
Ray Lewis	Linebacker	6'1"	240
J.J. Watt	Defensive End	6'5"	290
Anthony Muñoz	Lineman	6'6"	280

Wide Receivers

Wide receivers are exciting to watch. They line up on the sides of the field and race to get open. They can turn quickly and dash away from cornerbacks. They can jump high and stretch out long for catches. And they always keep their toes inside the sideline when catching the ball.

Randy Moss was tall and thin. His legs were so long that it looked like he was running in slow motion. But he could outrun anyone on the field. He was a threat to turn any catch into a touchdown.

Moss led the NFL in touchdown catches for five seasons, including his rookie year.

NFL Receiving Records

Most Catches	Most Yards	Most Receiving TDs, Career	Most Receiving TDs, Season
Jerry Rice, 1,549	Jerry Rice, 22,895	Jerry Rice, 197	Randy Moss, 23 (2007)
Larry Fitzgerald, 1,432	Larry Fitzgerald, 17,492	Randy Moss, 156	Jerry Rice, 22 (1987)

Jerry Rice was also fast and able to jump high. He was strong too. Rice could overpower cornerbacks and safeties to win the ball. He was a fierce **competitor.** In 20 years in the NFL, he played in a record 303 games.

Rice won three Super Bowls with the 49ers. He was named MVP of Super Bowl XXIII.

Tight Ends

The tight end lines up next to one of the tackles. On running plays, the tight end blocks for the running back, just like a lineman. On passing plays, he runs downfield and catches passes, just like a wide receiver.

The two greatest tight ends played at the same time. Antonio Gates played with the Chargers. Tony Gonzalez played most of his career with the Chiefs.

Both Gates and Gonzalez were college basketball players. Playing basketball gave them quick feet and good hands. They were also bigger than safeties and many linebackers. They could jump for catches, and they could power to the end zone for touchdowns.

GOAT Tight Ends

	Tony Gonzalez	Antonio Gates
Years	1997–2013	2003–2018
Catches	1,325	955
Yards	15,127	11,841
Touchdowns	111	116

Gonzalez carries the ball during a game against the Denver Broncos in 2003.

Gates makes a touchdown during a game against the Kansas City Chiefs in 2005.

Running Backs

Some running backs are small and speedy. Others are big and powerful. The two greatest running backs were very different in size.

Barry Sanders was small and quick. Even when defensive players had him trapped, he was able to stop, change directions, and slip away. He was MVP once and led the NFL in rushing yards four times. After only 10 seasons, he surprised everyone by retiring from the NFL.

Sanders was famous for long touchdown runs. His longest was 85 yards.

Jim Brown was big and powerful. When defensive players surrounded him, he knocked them down. Or he carried them. Brown also surprised everyone when he retired early. He played only nine seasons. He led the NFL in running yards eight times and was MVP three times.

Brown played 60 years ago, but he still holds many NFL records.

Running Back Records

Average Yards Per Game, Career	Average Yards Per Carry, Career	Most Games with More Than 150 Yards	Most TDs Longer Than 50 Yards
Jim Brown, 104.3	Jim Brown, 5.2	Barry Sanders, 25	Barry Sanders, 15
Barry Sanders, 99.8	Barry Sanders, 5	Jim Brown, 22	Jim Brown, 12

Quarterbacks

The quarterback is usually the biggest star on a team. Great quarterbacks can turn a losing team into a winning team. The greatest can bring a team to the Super Bowl.

The two greatest quarterbacks are Tom Brady and Peyton Manning. They were **rivals** who often played against each other. They are friends off the field. Who is the GOAT? You can decide.

Comparing Quarterback Records

Tom Brady's Records	Peyton Manning's Records
Most wins: 251	First quarterback to win 200 games
Most touchdown passes, career: 649	Most touchdown passes, season: 55
Most passing yards in a playoff game: 505	Most passing yards in a season: 5,477
Most Super Bowl MVP awards: 5	Most NFL MVP awards: 5
Most Pro Bowls: 15	

Brady was the second quarterback to lead two different teams to Super Bowl wins. He won six titles with the Patriots and a record seventh with the Buccaneers.

Manning was the first quarterback to lead two different teams to Super Bowl wins. He won first with the Colts. He won his second Super Bowl with the Broncos in his final game.

Glossary

blitz (BLITS)—to attack quickly; in football, when a linebacker, cornerback, or safety runs across the line to get the quarterback

career (kuh-REER)—all of the years a pro player spends playing a sport

competitor (kuhm-PEH-tuh-tuhr)—a person who is trying to win in a sport or game

complicated (KAHM-pluh-kayt-ed)—something that has many parts and is hard to understand

fearsome (FEER-sum)—frightening or scary

formation (for-MAY-shun)—in football, the way that players line up on offense and defense before the play starts

intercept (in-tur-SEPT)—to catch a pass the quarterback has thrown toward an offensive player when you're playing defense

line of scrimmage (LINE UHV SKRIM-ij)—the imaginary line across a football field that goes out from where the football is placed before a play begins; the offense and defense have to stay on their own side of the line before the play starts

rival (RYE-vuhl)—someone whom a person competes against

rookie (ROOK-ee)—a first-year player

Guide to Roman Numerals

The Super Bowls are counted using Roman numerals—the way that the ancient Romans wrote their numbers.

I = one
V = five
X = ten
L = fifty

To get the total number, you add each letter. Super Bowl XXXVII has three tens (XXX), a five (V), and two ones (II). If you add 10 + 10 + 10 + 5 + 1 + 1, that adds up to Super Bowl 37. An I before a V or an X means "one less," so IV is 4, and XXIX is 29.

Read More

Gramling, Gary. *The Football Fanbook*. New York: Time Inc. Books, 2017.

Hetrick, Hans. *Football's Record Breakers*. North Mankato, MN: Capstone, 2017.

Johnson, George. *NFL Heroes: The 100 Greatest Players of All Time*. Buffalo, NY: Firefly Books, 2020.

Internet Sites

Ducksters: "Football: National Football League"
https://www.ducksters.com/sports/national_football_league.php

NFL
nfl.com

Sports Illustrated Kids: "Football"
sikids.com/football

Index

About the Author

photo by Marta Berglund

Bruce Berglund is a writer and historian. For 19 years, he taught history at Calvin College and the University of Kansas. His courses included the history of China, Russia, women in Europe, sports, and war in modern society. He has earned three Fulbright awards and traveled to 17 countries for research and teaching. His most recent book is *The Fastest Game in the World*, a history of world hockey published by the University of California Press. Bruce works as a writer at Gustavus Adolphus College, and he teaches writing classes at the Loft Literary Center in Minneapolis. His four children grew up reading books from Capstone Press, especially the graphic novel versions of classic literature. Bruce grew up in Duluth and now lives in southern Minnesota.